# THREE POEMS

*poems by*

# Reginald Gibbons

*Finishing Line Press*
Georgetown, Kentucky

# THREE POEMS

Copyright © 2024 by Reginald Gibbons
ISBN 979-8-88838-740-5 First Edition
All rights reserved under International and Pan-American Copyright Conventions. No part of this book may be reproduced in any manner whatsoever without written permission from the publisher, except in the case of brief quotations embodied in critical articles and reviews.

Publisher: Leah Huete de Maines
Editor: Christen Kincaid
Cover Art: Reginald Gibbons
Author Photo: Reginald Gibbons
Cover Design: Elizabeth Maines McCleavy

Order online: www.finishinglinepress.com
also available on amazon.com

Author inquiries and mail orders:
Finishing Line Press
PO Box 1626
Georgetown, Kentucky 40324
USA

# Contents

Mōdor : An elegy ..................................................................................... 1

Mother Tongue ........................................................................................ 7

Elegy ....................................................................................................... 11

*I don't know if the riddle*
*Of the darkness after death is decipherable,*
*But life, like autumnal*
*Tranquility, is detailed to the infinitesimal.*

—Boris Pasternak ("Let's Let Words Fall")

# Mōdor : An Elegy

*É dificile dire con parole di figlio...* —Pasolini

Wordlessly you insisted on your aloneness and you never seemed to allow yourself to acknowledge what your own body, your own spirit, might confess to thinking, morning, afternoon and night.

Night—when you cried out sometimes from within your bad dreams.

Somewhere far away, reflected in slow bayous and rivers, were planets and stars.

Even as I began, when still a child, to sense what our mutual thinking felt like in my anxious gut, I still could not let go of what your being said to me without your having to say it, without you being able to say it. Certainly not wanting to say it. Yet I heard it.

Which is why now I can't help wanting to tell you something that you'll hear only inside me, where you can't hear it, but my sometimes dim and sometimes blinding projection of you still lives:

from your example, maybe, I built my own interior of protected places.

But that seemed to give me the sense that you were irreplaceable. Which was certainly wrong, but at the same time I had to admit to myself that although I had once been inside you and came out, you were still in me, even now.

As if in their own depths, slow-moving waters looked up and thought that it was the planets and stars that were wobbling.

Did you ever come to the surface of yourself? I have some appetite for what's below my usual sense of myself. And for what moves in those inner spaces. With a sudden impulse inward I headlamp my dives and stay in one underwater chamber or another till I adjust myself to what's obscure.

In there, I study a small vastness. I try to hold myself steady. Knowing you're the images painted on those submerged walls in ochre and black. I could float a while in my grottos, breathing only remembered air—storm scent, your potent colognes, and both the sweet and the pungent scents of the nearby weed fields where I wandered on my own, when small.

Also the acrid smell of the sun-softened asphalt of our road.

Despite my childhood escapes from you when I went deep into the pages of the used books you bought for me for a dime or a quarter each at the Good Will store, and later, despite my mature ear for subtleties of word-sounds and my eye for some images that I would rather not even have imagined, I could never, I never did, figure you well in words.

Your own journeys inward were forced on you by your lonely place in your family of origin, and then later you enforced them on the children you raised. You'd come from neglect and bullying and bewilderment. You excelled in shaming your offspring and husband.

You imagined, you attempted, a little career, but—and this was genuine misfortune—your few good chances were stolen by illness and by your own self-doubt and temperament, and even by the fig-leaf fashion in which you must have mated. By your losses, your bosses, your mistaken first marriage and then your decision to divorce, and then the forced quickness and deadness of your wartime second marriage, your second husband, in only a few months, who, having gained at your cost his right to remain in the United States, insisted on your second divorce.

"Thanks! *Köszönöm!*"—that guy may have said, or not. Whoever he was, I don't know, or maybe he said "*Poděkování!*"—I appreciate it! Because you'd done for him what he—not you—most needed. You'd gotten him his American status. And then—how bitterly this rebounded against you— you and your first husband, who, dispirited, returned from the war with his limbs intact, produced the inevitability of my birth, and the two of you had to remarry in order to legitimize me and avoid scandal. But thus you lost most of whatever you might otherwise have become.

Often you must have seen me as the ineradicable cause and proof of the inescapable error of your marriage to your first husband, who then became my father.

You worked and worked, at home and outside it. To the men who ran you in offices part-time you were useful. For bosses, although almost nobody else, you felt some admiration. This was later, while your children were in school and you worked part-time. They appreciated you. Grudgingly sometimes, your children did, too. Your smarts. Your energy. But the whippings: no, no, no, no.

Your precise psychological attacks were even worse than the physical ones: no, no, no, no.

You loved your oldest surviving brother, the violinist, but he considered you to be somewhat self-thwarting. You loved even more your oldest brother, but he died young. And your youngest brother, but he died even younger.

It was a long way to later life, and you fought it through to an impressively late end.

I can't believe you ever once got the kind of kiss that gives one a little more to live on. I don't think you ever gave such a kiss, either.

Ground meat, cabbage, eggs, pasta, jello, cake mixes, "ice milk," margerine, instant coffee, chickens we raised out back, and our garden tomatoes and beans and corn, the delivered bottles of milk, the black-&-white TV, the actor cowboys you loved, and by the time I was fourteen I had my learner's permit in our farm state and was driving you in your car to the A&P.

You might have thought that we all whispered and brooded, but we kept to ourselves everything you had done that pained us, physically or emotionally. Outwardly, we would have seemed well-tended prisoners. And we got old enough to be out and away with school friends.

If only you'd been more available, more generous, more compassionate. But probably never having felt anyone else's compassion for you, you had none of it to give to anyone else. Your self—like our selves—was what it had been made by others: vehement, wounded, disappointed, and ultimately left behind.

By me, at least.

You must have heard lots of inner noise. Underwater, sounds are so different. And there's no way to rejoice. Yet someone said that you felt wonder at your late first infant. (I.e.—I.)

I know, I know—almost all of you was about defending yourself against harms that you yourself had brought on.

Your subtlest sense of a slight, an affront, a disapproval, any unintended reminder from one of us that yes you were harsh, angry, disappointed, jealous, done with trying to get past everything that you'd pushed aside because you'd lived it or because you hadn't had the chance to live it—your subtlest sense of any of that often shoved you into a stark withdrawal. Shutting yourself in your own room, you'd remember your shoeless-in-summer, unkempt childhood near the three-trunked front-yard crepe myrtle—one with white, two with purple outbursts of blossoming tears.

On Cortlandt Street in the Heights, the heavy Houston rain, the weighty Houston heat, the fog or oil refinery stink that drifted in from the coast, flowing around the small frame houses. At its worst, it smelled of thousands of petroleum, fishy, bayou-polluted letdowns.

Your older sister—a pianist—died young in her bed of illness. Indirectly murdered, you told me, by her fiancé and his new girlfriend, who made her walk too far in the thin mountain air till her lungs bled within her and she died. Like your oldest brother—a great pianist—who, also still young, played and played and then collapsed. Terribly weak, wrapped in his bedsheets, as you and your mother sat beside his bed, in a hospital in New Orleans, at last he could no longer breathe. For years afterward, your mother played Chopin's "Raindrop" prelude again and again. Then you did. Then I did, too. And I still do.

Your kind second-oldest brother went away. In the war, your sweet youngest brother died very young. "A hero." Your mother put her soul on his honorary folded stars and stripes, sealed in a wide flat box left forever on her highest closet shelf. Her mind drifted into a confused and frightened theosophical fear and incompetence.

Your prettier younger sister, after she was done with husbands, died in a hospital.

Look, here they all are, in one of my inner cabinets of woeful curiosities, with your self-disapproval, self-discipline, self-justification, and formidable will.

And as I initiated my full fission from the real you, so as to gather as much energy as I could, and as I began to escape what you had tried to shape me to be, it was you, I think, who unwittingly taught me that your sense of what I should be was what I could not be satisfied with.

Against oneself, one may learn—with stealth and doggedness, and through lapses and regressions—to remain advantageously dissatisfied and to rethink everything, eventually, at least a little.

Or at least I thought everything was still in my head or my soul, but I never truly revisited it, because to do so pulled me back into the memories I wanted to escape.

I was changing what it was, for me, even if stubbornly so much of it wouldn't change. Won't. It. All of it. Your it—your life; my life, mine.

Later my heart took to beating crazily against its own wishes and well-being, against time and its own inner intimate staggering and weakness, letting me fall down dark shafts of my interior where water seeped constantly through earthen walls and stonework like that of a well shaft.

But just before I began to become a man, I got off the coastal plains and made it to the top of an unruined real space—a high western mountain peak, an incalculably immense rock, a high magnificent geological upheaval of all that is not human.

It gave me a view of more than a hundred-mile distance. But what was in the farthest distance could not be seen. Air—a hundred miles of it—over the earth is not transparent. (Nor are decades and decades of living.) And from that peak it seemed that hell had heights and heaven had depths. And from that peak in time I looked back, in my mind, eastward; I saw the crepe myrtle in bloom, I watched a streetcar grinding along Heights Boulevard, maybe in 1931 or '32.

Slowly it hissed and shrieked up Main Street and then you stepped down at that department store where you were a secretary for some manager. In dark skirt, white blouse, close-fitting jacket—all sewn by you. Maybe I could smile and wish you luck.

But you, knowing that you had little luck and weren't able to make much of it come to you, knowing that you were already caught without credible or even unwanted possibilities for yourself, trying to think of how to become more of yourself, wanting to make more use of your own untrained, uninformed, yet remarkable intelligence, understanding that whatever work you got would require you to defer to the men who bossed you, and to flatter them, knowing that you did not think you wanted children, and then learning that you too had TB, and having to stop your night-school art courses drawing dresses for newspaper fashion advertisements, you might have been panicked by the grim possibility that your talents would never be allowed any scope, that you might never receive the training you deserved, and that you too might die in bed when still in your twenties, like your older sister and brother… or your youngest brother, who had made a willing, fatal, heroic sacrifice during the War.

Biting your lower lip, wearing that intensely guarded look that was you, glancing at the people swaying on the streetcar, not wanting to be glanced at, sweating in the hot summer morning….

I'll keep looking back across the years before you bore me, even though it's impossible to do so.

But maybe I'll catch sight of you on the street car on your way to work. If I do, I'll offer you my seat but you won't know who I am.

*3/16/2017—3/20/2017—6/25/2020—2/26/2023*

## Mother Tongue

        Please, if you possibly can,
dear blow-soft, breathe-hard lingo,
        our all-you-can-say noun-hound
with verbal wrist, twist open

        your breath-spigot of true words!
And pardon me please, dear Mom-
        tongue, for not yet having vir-
tuoso'd my lexicon

        of your truths as I beat back
false utterance, and while you're
        here, would you give us please a
boisterous curse on evil-

        mouthed scam-minded sham-Caesar
word-salads of lies, malign
        designs, and payoffs of fraud?
First, our despotic lover

        of lucre and mayhem, our
gold-plate dodger and under-
        little-hander-in-chief, skin-
color-crazed flagbearer of

        flags all false. He who can tell
no truth-hood nor say good sooth,
        he who yowls and bays his cur-
scurrilous heart-fanging false-

        hoods and hatred! If only,
Mother, you yourself could de-
        fend *yourself* against our loud-
mouthing hatemonger! Such a

        moral swindler, such an all-
ways-has-been-slanderer, thug,
        grifter—surrounded by his
adoring minions, bloody-

minded insurrectionists.
His delight in stirring up
red hornets' nests of angry,
hate-roiling solo warriors

in love with their guns and in
hate with all who ask for help,
speak other languages, and
ask for what is theirs to claim

rightfully. Please, please, Mama,
throw the light of true telling
across our plains and poisoned
waters and mined mountains, our

poor towns and jerrymandered
districts, our factories of
weapons, our poisoned approved
projects that crush what is good

and inflate mentalities
of vehemence, virulence,
viciousness, brutality.
Please don't let them all keep bull-

pooping in your well, please bell
them, repel them, don't make us
have to smell their foul mouths spew
bilious hatred, bad faith, sick

plans of harm. Please shut their gobs,
expose their lies, delicts, and
fantasies of lawlessness.
Whack their tongues, correct their syc-

ophancy, gag their smirking
rants, their love of muscle and
of being ruled, their rank fraud
of a fascist God. Help us

                clap shut their arrant, foul, pest-
ilent blather and braying!
                    Would you slap down their über-
flapping right-feathering-wing

                flapdoodle? Will you help bust
their tyranno-thesaurus
                of slurs and malice and threats,
their maniacal hurrahs,

                their phantasms of brute harm,
the lightless dungeon of what
                they would impose. Saboteurs
of reason, egoists of

                autarchy, they'd choose to splash
everyone with far-worse-than-
                (both) Bush politics of bomb-
lit Biblically bloody

                petro-oases. Mother,
please! Verity would so help!
                Let's speak truth to folly—for
the Tyrant tries to save his

                own neck from yester-crimes of
selling his country out and
                wrecking our house divided.
Deplorables devastate

                lives, care, aid. They would outlaw
compassion. They'd argue for
                selling off our embassies
(for dictators—secret dis-

                counts! For classified papers—
free copies!), Putinizing
                skies, our rivers, our love, our
truth. Our own oligarchs say

           they *care*—while stealing the sea
from whales, forests from fauna,
           rain from farm fields and lakes, while
others pump viral choler

           and bile into wrathful, self-
deluding, stiff-saluting
           psyches. They'll seethe and rant in
favor of fracking Eden;

           they'll watch our cities drown… You've
got to help us, Mom!—even
           with those self-willed, suspect high
judges who deploy their cold

           Latinate legalese to
pronounce their verdicts from be-
           neath their secular cassocks….

# ELEGY

(Written by hand in the top & side & bottom margins—29 May 1996—
& including the first line of poetry on each page of
*The Cantos of Ezra Pound,*)

## THE CANTOS OF EZRA POUND
In 1971, when my graduate classes ended in the spring, I was going to leave for Europe for the first time. I was working on a PhD in Comparative Literature, & M. & I were planning a year abroad, made possible by a Fulbright fellowship I'd been awarded for study in Spain & an unexpected gift of $1500 from my Uncle Dan, the violinist (on my mother's side), who evidently wanted to help someone from my family get a sense of life elsewhere.

## A NEW DIRECTIONS BOOK
My wife M. & I were living in a tiny redwood cottage. My fellow student & friend from undergraduate days, the poet N., then also a fellow graduate student, was going to sublet our cottage for the year. My friend F.—he too a PhD student in English, & like N., also one who wrote poems—asked if he could borrow some of my poetry books for

## CONTENTS
as long as M. & I would be gone. I was happy that my fellow poets N.—who would get

### A Draft of XXX Cantos (1930)
the benefit of our tiny house (one bookcase, a mattress on the floor, a miniature kitchen, & wooden casement windows painted yellow, with no screens—& F., some of my books

### Eleven New Cantos XXXI-XLI (1934)
while we were away. In the midst of newly

### The Fifth Decad of Cantos XLII-LI (1937)
met poets & fiction writers among my fellow students & future scholars,

### Cantos LII-LXXI (1940)
I had found F. especially congenial. He was getting

### The Pisan Cantos LXXIV-LXXXIV (1948)
a PhD in English. I might

### Section: Rock-Drill De Los Cantares LXXXV-XCV (1955)
have met him through D.—she & I were in the same Old

### Throne de los Cantares XCVI-CIX (1959)
English course. F. & I became close friends—we played

### Drafts and Fragments of Cantos CX-CXVII (1969)
chess (badly), talked poetry & translation, & didn't much discuss how far the elite university that was giving us fellowships was extending our journey away from our unremarkable origins. It was a place hallowed, too, at least in its own view, by the spirit of the late Yvor Winters, the formidably opinionated poet & critic. Would we become as certain as he in our views of anything, given our sense that we were entering carefully this hallowed precinct as cultural immigrants who had worked our way in & up? Donald Davie—a brilliant & learned conservative poet & critic who had migrated to California partly to escape both English cultural insularity & leftist radicalism on English campuses—had replaced Winters. How could we ever impress *him*? (I was at numerous student demonstrations.)

\*

Like me, F. was from a half-immigrant family—his in New Jersey, mine in Texas. His father drove a cab. Mine drove an old Chevy, then later a small Japanese truck on his sales rounds to small independent grocery stores. There was sorrow in F's family of origin. Unhappiness & sometimes violence in mine. As a grad student, F. lived in a little rented cottage in an old, unharvested apricot orchard, up a hill somewhere south of campus, & a number of grad students used to gather there for dinner sometimes, cook pasta & chickens, smoke weed, drink cheap local wine, talk, sort out constellations as we lay on our backs after dinner on the dry-season ground, on the comfortable slope of the orchard—

\*

Once, in the spring of 1970, it might have been, F. & I were standing at midnight in a small park next to the house that M. & I had rented—the front part—in our first Californian year—before we moved to a cheaper, very small, redwood cottage a few blocks away—& with a flashlight that we had covered with red cellophane so we could read the star guide & not lose our night vision (where did we get red cellophane?)

### A DRAFT OF
& two cops in a patrol car spotlit us & interrogated us

## XXX CANTOS

from the street with their bullhorn & we had to explain what we were doing. They laughed at us. White-haired old Mrs. S., our landlady that first year, lived behind M. & me in the back part of her house, quite separately from us, with a small backyard garden of fig & persimmon trees, vegetables, flowers (a simple archetype of garden & benign sky & earth, & right behind it lay the Southern Pacific tracks along which the locomotives & cars of both passenger & freight trains passed so close & so loud that they shook the house & overwhelmed our voices). When Mrs. Schneider decided to put in a small patio for her renters, I offered to do the job for her. Perhaps she gave us back some of that month's rent, which was $130 a month in 1969-70. I recruited F. & we dug out the ground, filled the space with sand & laid square cement flagstones into place, leveling them carefully.

*

Decades later, in 1994, C. & I went to San Francisco together, & one day we rented a car & drove to Palo Alto. Highway 101 had become like the New Jersey Turnpike, not the almost bucolic highway—if such a thing is possible— that it had been in the 70s, with

**And then went down to the ship,**
flowering vines along the median. I drove us to Mrs. S.'s house; it & the adjacent small park seemed completely unchanged. We walked slowly up the driveway with respectful caution,

**Men many, mauled with bronze lance heads,**
& I saw a very old white-haired woman come out of the door of the back portion of the house—& it was she, still amazingly like herself as she had been more than twenty years earlier. I called her name almost in disbelief, & then we ended up

**"Shalt return, through spiteful Neptune, over dark seas…"**
talking for a while. Having rented out that front part of her house so many times, she did not remember me. Everything, even the fig trees, seemed unchanged, although the garden seemed less lush than my memory of it. F.'s patio—I felt that somehow it was more his than mine—was worn but in excellent shape. A low anonymous monument to our tall youth. Had F. already known how to do this? I had known, from one such earlier job. It was only a patio.

\*

F. learned of a hiking route up Black Mountain, the tallest of the Santa Cruz Mountains, between Palo Alto & the coast. Fog flowing in from the ocean sometimes rose high enough to push

**Hang it all, Robert Browning,**
long exploratory fingers or tendrils up through the passes, & down the dips between the hills—a benign white invading form, completely

**Snipe come for their bath,**
organic in appearance, like a growing thing, that came over & down a bit toward the valley of the bay. On a sunny dry hot summer day, F. & I drove up to a high property he knew of—what was the name?—something Ranch?—& we

**Sea-break from stern forrards,**
parked the car—his or mine—& we took

**Olibanum is my incense,**
the trail he knew that led to the summit of Black Mountain, on top of which there were transmitting antennas. From where we began hiking, the path rose through fragrant eucalyptus stands & laurel groves & up rocky places, across meadows & pastures. Up & up—a fabulous landscape— that is, of some fable that we did not know. A landscape that made one want to write

**Black azure and hyaline,**
Poundian poems, a landscape of Mediterranean dry sunny heat, stillness, in the chapparal the odors of dry weeds & herbs, under a sky in which the sun did seem to have been a living god in some earlier time. The trail went through fields, brush, & pasture. At one point, warily, slowly, we walked at a distance from a bull—it too from the ancient fable inside which we were still present. We didn't have to clamber through or over any fences, for there were cattle guards, not gates, in the ground wherever the dirt roads up

**I sat on the Dogana's steps**
there crossed a fence line. We hiked upward for two hours or so. We saw no one else going up or coming down. From the top, we beheld the spectacular view of history—the bay, the roads, the long-ago Native life & then enslaving settlers from Spain, followed by brutal conquest by the United States: more slavery, murder, kidnapping of children. F. & I spotted a coyote on a hill below, loping easily through high wild grasses.

**With no hawks left there on their perches,**
Not an extremely clear view, because of the summer
haze from air pollution, & perhaps dust, in a long season of drought, but
nevertheless a view better than it was to be in the future. We sat at the top a
while, talking, looking, thinking a bit about poems—not ours but those of
the greats, alive & dead—& then hiked down again—harder on my bad knees
than the climbing had been—& we drove to a house where there was
a swimming pool—friends of friends—& for a while the pool
relieved me of soreness in my muscles, joints, bookish spirit.
In the spring of 1971, M. & I packed for our long trip, bought a used VW
"squareback" to serve as our traveling storage locker—we were going by
freighter—& we left N. & his girlfriend the little house, & I loaned F. some
books of his choice:

**Palace in smoky light,**
poems. Among them, an especially prized possession, the first edition of
the complete text of Pound's *Cantos* (1970). M. & I left in May for the East
Coast, then on the ship for Yugoslavia, then Turkey, then Spain, where we
stayed until September of the next year.

**'Tis. 'Tis. Ytis!**
When we returned to our redwood cabin, we began to put things in order
again, & F. brought back the books he had borrowed. I don't recollect now
anything about any of them except this one,

**Stumbling, stumbling along in the wood,**
this very one, in which today, May 29, 1996, I have

**No wind is the king's wind.**
begun writing this brief recollection.

**Great bulk, huge mass, thesaurus;**
There was now a very peculiar thing about this

**"In satieties…"**
book—& I was baffled by it &

**Click of the hooves, through garbage,**
dismayed. The appearance of

**Prods the Pope's elephant, & gets no crown, where Mozarello**
the book—which had been pristine when I had given
it to F.—shocked me. The dust jacket was tattered, & now,
ineffectually protected by a yellowing plastic cover.
The page-edges were dirty. I stop writing in it now with my pen &
I hold it & turn it & can tell from looking at the edges
that F. worked more in the "Pisan Cantos" than
in anything else—darkened by repeated
use of those pages—use which would
have been immensely interesting
to me, but inside, the worst
discovery: F. had written

**What you have done, Odysseus,**
comments in pencil on many many pages. It was the sort of study
& annotating which, in those days before detailed scholarly guides to
this massive compendium, one simply had to do it oneself, in order to grasp
a fraction, a mere fraction, of what Pound had been up to.
It was not the penciled marginalia that disturbed
me but an opposite aspect: after F.'s immense amount of research &
annotating—such dedicated & invaluable aid to study, to appreciation,
to the complex

**"Need not wed Alix… in the name"**
back-&-forth of reading this kind of allusive, elusive, fragmented stuff—

**"free of person, free of will"**
F. had erased (!) all his annotations, & the deliberate & indelible
erasure—so to speak—of all that negating effort startled & perplexed me.
& why hadn't he just kept the book, with its virtually palimpsestic depths,
& bought me a new copy? This book was not hard to find, in those days, &
in those days there was such a richness of literary bookstores that getting
another *Cantos* would have been easy.
I would have bought a new copy for myself—& I dearly wished that I could
have read all his annotations. He did not, & would not, tell me why he'd
erased it all. I'd have photocopied those pages & given
the book to him. Was his—& my—purchase on Pound's word

**Eleanor (she spoiled in a British climate)**
so inadequate that it must be erased? His notes must have been brilliant. He
was brilliant. My book was restored to me, with his apologies

**We also made ghostly visits, and the stair**
for all the traces of his pencilings & for the generally shabby state of
the object. Its worn appearance upset me, as did his expunged insights &
questions, which had been erased as if to make certain to leave plentiful
smudges—signs of

**Lamplight at Buovilla, e quel remir,**
their once having been there. & they'd been removed with sufficient
force not to leave anything legible, which

**Lies heavy in my arms, dead weight**
was much more disturbing than the sheer wear on the pages, because I
would have been so pleased to have been able to benefit from all
of his study, his hours upon hours of intellectual labor! Ah—"The live man,"
Pound writes on this page, "...probes for old wills & friendships."

**These fragments you have shelved (shored).**
For a long while I didn't use the book or even look at it.

**But I want it to be quite clear, that until the chapels are ready**
Nor did I want a new copy. Or if I did,

**Of these 50,000 florins, free of attainder,**
but didn't buy one, anyway, I suppose I wrongly preferred

**With the sheets spread from windows,**
to hold onto my irritation—keeping it alive like a subtle

**With the church against him,**
ache—& I should have chosen the simple remedy of giving this

**And the dusk rolled / to one side a little**
book back to him who had made & unmade its layers of attention.
All this was so long ago that perhaps it's odd that I recall anything at all of it.
But I do recall this incident of, as I think now, a kind of sorrow
of self-denial. That's the theme, perhaps, of which this copy of the book
is the evidence. Only now is the theme clear to me—he couldn't resist the
pleasure of studying & annotating the book (& who could?), & then felt he
had defaced it, & so wanted to remove the defacement but instead left another
kind on the page. I didn't understand this, then. & although F.'s life ended
years ago—even the small narrative that I know—

**One year floods rose,**
it is not at all a theme of self-defeating,

**through the wangle of the Illus. Sgr. Mr. Fedricho d'Orbino**
because

**And old Foscari wrote,** *"Caro mio"*
F. succeeded brilliantly

**And Feddy finally said "I am coming!..."**
in many ways. But it's one of those movements

**"father's opinium that he has shode to Mr. Genare about the"**
of a spirit that turns back—I imagine—to confront itself. When I knew
him in those early years, perhaps

**boss to fix up that wall to the little garden that madame Isotta**
he was unable ever to be satisfied

**ILLUSTRIOUS PRINCE:**
that he had done enough, & done it well enough, & out of that feeling came an

**That's what they found in the post-bag**
impulse to destroy work that he may have thought he had done insufficiently
well, rather than let it stand. (& erased some things he wanted
to show me about the poem? or erased all that to hide from me what he may
have thought was inadequate?) After all, despite his intellectual brilliance &
his genuine poetic gift, his responsiveness to poems, to poetry's ways
of meaning, he made a long slow haul of completing
his own study of poetry, & his own poems. Was his nature, his temperament,
a perfectionism vulnerable to disillusionment & to abandoning its object?
He showed me few poems, or none, after those early
years of our friendship—& I thought he must have stopped writing, entirely.
It's painful to think about this, about him,

**And the poor devils dying of cold, outside Sorano**
& I realize that I'm avoiding this remembrance instead of other aspects &
events of California years. Although in the early 1970s, old-timers like Mrs. S.
could not help saying: "You should have seen it all

**And he said:** *"Caro mio,* **I can not receive you"**
ten years ago!" Or twenty. Yet unwittingly we were only

**ET SCRIPTURA EX ORE PRODIIT, QUAE DICERET:**
another generation of future old-timers who would point backward into
the mirages & calamities of the past

**That he might in God's dishonour**
& say—You should have seen it around 1970... In Palo
Alto, on the corner of El Camino

**God's enemy and man's enemy,** *stuprum, raptum*
Real & the Oregon Expressway, where horses were pastured behind
barbed-wire fencing, hotels would later be built,
but before that, sometimes several

**And they said: Novvy'll sell any man**
horses would stand at the corner as if thinking about the traffic. Kenneth
Patchen was living in a tract house nearby, in intractable pain.
(But I never thought to try to visit him. I should have.
But why would he want to be called on by me?)
A friend of his told me about him—she was perhaps sixty, the secretary
of the Comparative Literature program. (Mrs. Barnes, I remember you
& thank you for kindnesses.) She also told me of having lived for
many years up in the big hills, on Skyline Drive, on a big property from
which, at one particular spot, one could see a silver sliver of the Pacific
(which for eons had scarcely been used by human beings & then became
industrialized into a salt-water cistern of toxins, trash, dying populations of
creatures, bad weather, & oil tanker routes). Mrs. Barnes told me she had
once seen a female cougar cross open ground in front of her house, followed
by amusingly clumsy cubs. Such moments could make one feel pleasurably
hidden, fantasizing the natural world for a moment, in some long-ago era, &
yet there had been such trauma & suffering, & fewer pleasurable decades or
centuries than would ever be replicated.

**EGRADMENT** *li antichi cavaler romanj*
After Mrs. Barnes' husband had died, she was forced by need to
sell that home & wilderness & then, a few years later, missing

**I mean Sidg went to Tarentum**
that place very much, she had gone up there again to
inquire about repurchasing just the house, without all

**And an old woman came in and giggled to see him**
the surrounding acreage, & the owner, the one to whom she herself had sold

**Yes, I saw him when he was down here**
it, told her—"You'll never have enough money to buy it."

**And one day he said: Henry, you can have it**
So—in that extraordinary place: our classes, poetry
workshops, group dinners, chess while
sitting outside in soft shade, evenings in the orchard
where a lion might pass in the dark,

**And we sit here under the wall**
& in perfect air of summer mornings when the weather was
neither too hot

**Commercial stationery,**
nor rainy, when the outdoors seemed as still as an
immense, flower-scented, light-drenched

**Porkers, throughout all Portugal,**
room, when I worked at weak poems in the quiet late morning alone,
with—at that time, still, an ingrained Protestant expectation of
reward for difficult mental toil....

**Said Jim X....:**
Probably because of Donald Davie—so productive, so confident
when with us, or we with him, keeping his doubts about himself,
& about us, too, to himself—whom we were chasing in vain,

**"You called me your father, and I ain't"**
artistically, at that time (& with whom we never caught up). My fellow
grad student G., also from England, was another of Davie's best,
& G. & F. & I would talk from time to time of Donald's canny
meetings with us, one by one, in which he seemed to each of us a different
thinker, as he put himself in the role of that teacher
whom each student needed. (& would we have wanted to see
ourselves as he saw us?) There was a fruitful complexity, even
self-contradiction, of attitudes in him that far outstripped

**Kung walked by the dynastic temple**
in maturity what G. or F. or I could do when so young, or
perhaps ever would do. Davie's example especially challenged us,
precisely because we did not

**For Yuan Jang sat by the roadside pretending to be receiving wisdom.**
share his conservative political & religious views. & perhaps
we were unable to equal his honesty of self-scrutiny about them. "But let me
not luxuriate in self-reproach," he'd say sometimes.

**And Kung said "Wan ruled with moderation,"**
So naturally, when the time came for F.
to write a dissertation, Donald directed it (& mine, as well, & G's).
But not on Pound—for F. had now shifted his
interest & poetic allegiances to Auden & Horace, poets far
saner than EP. Those two polished, self-possessed minds
(as they shaped themselves in their poems, anyway)
became for F. the models of a decorum (& urbane
detachment, perhaps?) that suited F.'s needs far better than the cranky,
eccentric, passionate, arrogant, unpleasant, disturbing,
malevolent Ezra Pound, or the working-class worlds in which both F.& I had
been formed (he Catholic, & I Protestant).

**Io venni in luogo d'ogni luce muto;**
In 1974 I completed my graduate work—my translations of
Luis Cernuda
(& the critical introduction & notes). I'd been protected by Davie from

**the blowing of dry dust and stray paper,**
the very apparent hostility toward me of the director of my degree program.

**the vice-crusaders, fahrting through silk**
M., having worked in archives, accepted the offer of
a curatorial position in the east,
& she was very pleased about it, & I too, for her,

**The saccharescent, lying in glucose,**
& meanwhile, without my knowing it, Davie had arranged for me to be
offered part-time teaching of undergraduate creative

**Andiamo! One's feet sunk,**
writing classes. But M.'s full-time opportunity was more
important for her than the lectureship

**And the shield tied under me, woke**
could ever have been for me, & if I couldn't find work near hers, we could
live on her income for a while, we wouldn't need much, whereas we
could not have lived off mine, & she would have had to give up
her chance. So we sold our furniture, my upright piano, too, & we
packed the little else we owned into one big wooden crate to be shipped, &
we sold our leaky old Chevelle for $250 to a refugee from Chile who was
about to send for his wife to join him in the USA. (Salvador Allende had been
assassinated & his government had been overthrown by the Chilean military.)
Graduating friends were trying to disperse into the scarce chances of the
academic economy.

**And before hell mouth; dry plain**
F. & D. left together, as did G. & his wife C.—all four of whom I
had loved as friends & good companions, in shared cheer
& gloom, political bewilderment & vehement disgust & despair at needless
war, revolts, elections that changed most things for the worse. For several
more years F. worked on his dissertation while

**And I bathed myself with the acid to free myself of the hell ticks**
studying law. There were so few jobs in teaching.

**rising, spreading their garlands,**
His restless perfectionism was a boon,

**And they looked at it, and I can still hear the old admiral,**
he was older & focused,

**While he was out in the privy,**
I reckoned, better at law than the students fresh
out of their Bachelor's degrees, & F. was brilliant; & at this best
of schools he succeeded splendidly,

**Qu'est-ce que ça vaut, les généraux, le lieutenant**
he "made" the law review, & D. got a one-year postdoctoral
appointment & a leave from her new job to go

**C't homme, un type comme ça!**
where he was, & they were together a year, he got his law
degree & after his summer work

**And when it broke, there was the crowd there,**
he was offered a position at a formidable, high-dollar Manhattan firm &

**So that the vines burst from my fingers**
to break him in—as I saw it, anyway—

**In the suavity of the rock, cliff green-gray in the far,**
his superiors put him on the defense team for a whopping corporation that

**Guiding her with oar caught over gunwale, saying:**
had been sued in a class action by a multitude of victims

**"For this hour, brother of Circe."**
of asbestosis, sickened & killed by the callous company
policy, over decades, of withholding warnings of
the dangers of asbestos from anyone who worked with it, so as not to have to
provide either protection against the danger or compensation
for the damage. Soon F. was making frequent trips to London on
the Concorde, with senior colleagues, to the main
offices of that international regime of removing
oxygen from their workers' lungs. F. was also commuting

**And of Kublai:**
back & forth between Manhattan & D.'s university town on weekends (not all

**And old Biers was out there, a greenhorn,**
weekends) but sometimes D. would join him in Manhattan,

**A fine pair of giraffes to the nation,**
& once they came to visit M. & me on a summer Sunday.

**And I said: "They ain't heard his name yet."**
F. had brought with him some trial transcripts. When he told me what
task the firm had given him—& I heard what it had done to him already in
order to fit him for service to corporate dominion—I asked him,
"Can you do that?" This was,

**Sabotage? Yes, he took it up to Manhattan,**
after all, F.—the brilliant deep reader, thinker, literary scholar,
poet, stargazer. "Do what?" was

**corner reading The Tatler,**
the gist & pith of his reply. I can quite clearly hear
his voice & see his smile. His dazzling quickness. "Listen
to this! Listen to this!" he said. He flipped the broad pages of the transcripts of
trial testimony that he was studying

**Like they had, just *had*, to have the hemp via Rotterdam.**
& he read to me some exchanges between the attorneys for
the sick plaintiffs & the

**So I said to the X. and B. Central,**
corporate defense litigators.

**In the houseboats, with the turquoise.**
"They don't know the law! They're ridiculous!"—
he said, smiling, snorting with his good-natured impatience at the less
competent lawyers who were arguing for the feeble, wheezing, ex-laborers. "If
their attorneys don't know the law, they don't
deserve to win the case," he said. "That's
what it's about, not who's right & who's wrong."
Mission accomplished, re: F., by the high legal representatives of
ownership, & I couldn't help thinking he was glad to have
risen quickly. He was changing. So was I. He had changed
the spelling of his last name to make it

**Sound slender, quasi tinnula,**
more easily assimilated in his new waspy world,

**"You know for seex mon's of my life"**
(an edginess that I too felt)—less a sign of an only recent

**And came here, condit Atesten...**
access to the stations of an institution like his law firm. That day,
I thought that our friendship—I was afraid—was so suddenly
attenuated, or so breached, by this political dissonance,

**Wilderness of renewals, confusion**
& by our several years already of drifting apart, from lack

### D'amore mi mise, nel fuoco d'amore mi mise
of contact, that I felt uneasy, at a loss, & disappointed in
myself for feeling this.

### "And lie by night with the goddess?"
Even though I loved them both, & M. & I saw them other times.

### Head in arm's curve, reclining;
Once, at Thanksgiving—we took the train & stopped to stay
with them, on our way further south to Orlando to visit M.'s
grandmother, & I bought a lot of books in a used bookstore in Durham.

### "Keep the peace, Borso!" Where are we?
I discovered—while in D.'s car on the way to the train station—that I

### And from '34 when I count it, to last year,
had mistakenly left our tickets inside one of the books that I had already
boxed & mailed home. Had I unconsciously wanted
to stay longer with them?

### In your ordinary intercourse with your people to find out
But it was not much trouble

### Night of the golden tiger
to buy new tickets & then, later, to return the originals, unused, for a refund.
Nothing disturbing. Only my embarrassment. But also my living too much
in memories?—rather than in the changed friendship that I wanted to mend?

### Moon on the palm-leaf, confusion
At another time, we visited them in D.'s parents' house in Westchester
(posh by the standards of my keenly class-attuned formation, but really just
an ordinarily expensive pleasant suburban house on an unprepossessing,
thus exclusive & possessive, dirt road, with a

### An' that man sweat blood
swimming pool). F. convinced me, with his somehow vulnerable
cheer, to go with him on his regular

### The economist consulted of nations, said:
two-mile run, & amazingly to me, I, who never ran, completed it, fulfilled it,
somehow strengthened by his encouragement,

**And a voice behind me in the street.**
through green woods & up & down hill, cross-country, & on returning

**Be sefen an' seex for the summons**
to the house—no doubt at a slower pace than he would have
set if he had run alone (tall, he was a very

**And in came the elders and the scribes**
graceful, swift runner, with a long-legged, fluid gait)—

**And the judge says: Don't you know you aren't allowed all those buttons?**
we went into the pool for a swim, just like that time in California after hiking
down from Black Mountain—it was a kind of balm for all aches, physical
& psychical, & I emerged in no pain to a happy supper. & now
by some swift train of unheeded under-thought I cannot
know, I think of Davie again. Evading thoughts
of F.? Finding something needed, in a thought
of Donald? He—from a modest but literate
family in a Yorkshire coal-mining town
was very brilliant—"an athlete of
the examination hall" was how, in his full

**"Et omniformis," Psellos, "omnis"**
maturity, he described himself when he'd been a student, according to one of
the obituaries I read after he died in late 1995, a few years after F. had
died (at the age Donald had been, as F.'s mentor, & mine, & G.'s). I do not

*potì Bénthea*
doubt that Donald considered F. a deep-thinking student.
F. was passionate for learning &

**And he went out to Tierci, a jongleur**
he had a great memory—& thinking hard sometimes made him smile.

**Thus the book of the mandates:**
F. had been eager to study &

**arranging dot for Margarita his sister, to**
to study diligently & to school himself in manners & mores

**"Here Christ put his thumb on a rock"**
not his own by formation (as I was, too), creating in

**That was a judge of the court and noble,**
ourselves a new sense of being in some ways free,
& both of us saw Donald as mildly alien & Pound as alien & Winters'
work as alien (as F. & I were alien to Davie &
would have been to Pound)

**And it was the leaf of a diary**
& we studied them in order to test ourselves more deeply, to search
out the "piths & gists" & use them anew, in our own ways,

**THE BOOK OF THE COUNCIL MAJOR**
to learn how to be in contrast to them as well as in selective
emulation—how to read, how to think about
the poetic & political metabolism of our own culture, our own

**and in the said millessimo and month on a Sunday**
era, how to admire what was good, how to disagree with angry & sometimes
frightening righties & lefties. We hadn't thrown fists & stones like those that
had flown around us at demonstrations against &
supporters of the Vietnam war & Nixon & his minions again & again.

**being covered. To be revoked at the council's pleasure**
What to make now of our inner efforts then?

**Lay there, the long soft grass,**
Pound's poetry was open to all kinds of
materials & methods, yet it used that openness to close
something. Many things. What temperaments more
different from Pound's could F. have settled on for his deep
understanding of such poets as Horace & Auden?

**And against this the flute: pone metum,**
Perhaps it was an apprehensiveness about

**In 1513 on the last day of May was conceded to**
foreclosed opportunities, suffering, self-alienation, chaos (which I
only imagine, knowing almost nothing of it) in
the life F. had left behind, or

27

**And I came here in my young youth**
his admiration for Auden & Horace was perhaps for him a way into speaking
of pain with a polished confidence & irony.
& Pound himself had been for each of us an open gate into
an elevated cultural life that neither of us had been given.

**And you would have bust your bum laughing**
He had wanted his life to change & to stay changed—this F. whom
I knew & whom I now perhaps imagine as much
as remember. I was glad that he so enjoyed D. advising

**March 8, "That Sigismundo left Mantua"**
him as he picked out his law-firm Brooks Brothers suits, shirts,

**What yr. ldP [1 pound] wants me to buy**
& shoes. I remember his broad smile—

**To the Marquis of Mantova, Fran° Gonzaga**
like a boy's—as he let her tell of how, when they

**To the supreme pig, the archbishop of Salzburg:**
were choosing a pair of wing-tip

**Formando di disio nuova persona**
brogues, F. had asked for three identical pairs of them.

**1908, 1909, 1910, and there was**
"If you find what you want," he said, "why look any further?"

**Brumaire, Fructidor, Petrograd**
& he flourished in his legal career.

**Saying: "Me Cadmus sowed in the earth"**
Meanwhile, Davie had left Stanford & gone to

**And God the Father Eternal (Boja d'un Dio!)**
Vanderbilt, which meant in effect he

**In pale indeterminate colours.**
was leaving behind once again, as he'd done when he left England for
America, what

**Leaving the lady who loved bullfights**
he certainly felt had been a degree of

**And continued with hope of degrees and**
unmanageability in the chaos of the then

**only highest type will be included,**
highly politicized (some had guns) & activist student life of the

**Uniform out for Peace Day**
sixties & seventies, & since the sheer

**And when the Prince Oltrepassimo died, saccone,**
momentum of the already extended sixties was continuing—especially

**But for the night saw neither sky nor ocean**
in northern California, where nature because of
its clemency was such a perfect theater for demonstrations & public
pronouncements by placard or chant. After F. & I & other students
moved on, Davie withdrew himself to an inland American province
(for greater devotion to Christian verse & practice, as I saw it) & away from
his former protégés. I don't know, though, if F.
even sought—as I did (but I mostly failed)—
to maintain contact with our former mentor. (Who had been, when we
knew him, our model of how to combine the writing of poetry, at a level of

**PEARL, great sphere, and hollow,**
the highest artistic goals & highest cultural stakes, however
poorly the age responded to them, with energetic

**In the house of the Cavalcanti**
thinking & feeling, but of a somewhat skeptical kind—that is,
for the purpose of making judgments. This did not serve, though,
for the purpose of loving. None of us that I know of from that time,

**By the lawn of the senior elder**
at least, has ever or will ever come close to

**The mythological exterior lies on the moss in the forest**
the sheer intelligence & insight in Davie's secular thought—in his

**Nom de Dieu, et encore des valeurs.**
*Purity of Diction* & his book on syntax. But to me, "purity" remains a vicious
& suspect idea & so as Davie faded from our thinking,
the expanding time-universe

**Glide of water, lights and the prore,**
of the heart widened the gaps between our stars.
In some years, I taught writing workshops for two weeks in North Carolina
not terribly far from where D. & F. & their two small
daughters lived. (F., disappointed not to have found
a position teaching law there, was still commuting from—
rather than to—Manhattan.) Feeling a nostalgia for
that friendship, & perhaps guilt, that even though I was

**Compleynt, compleynt I hearde upon a day,**
not so far from them, & was very busy, during those two-week stays,

**After Ignez was murdered.**
& I was not letting these old friends know that I might have seen them again,

**from that of Messire Laurentius**
so three times I did arrange with D. to visit,

**Tempus loquendi, Tempus tacendi.**
three Januaries, but I found that twice, my arrivals

**in hopes you will find us returned to sentiments**
did not match weekends when F. was

**in Europe whose talents or merits would entitle him**
home from Manhattan—from work which, D. said, still excited & pleased him.

**"And must break I the chain of my thoughts to"**
So I visited with D. & met the little girls, & saw the things D. pointed
out to me as evidence of F.'s love of home—like

**"The revolution," said Mr. Adams,**
their small pond & a handsome bench beside it. & once that I recall

**that I carry into my retirement the highest veneration…**
in those several years, F. was there—an early visit in the sequence, I think, &

**AGATHOS, eternal and self-existent**
we sat in their living room, & the conversation,

**armies in this furious snow storm**
although I (& perhaps not only I) was eager for it, felt

**unfortunate labourers to their humanitarian fantasies**
somewhat awkward as I tried to recover the ease &

**yearly, merely in usurious discounts…**
comfortable unguardedness of years ago, but could not recover that ease.

**Oils, beasts, grasses, petrifactions, birds, incrustations**
Then a few years later, there came a call from D.

**"The fifth element: mud," said Napoleon.**
to tell me that F. was very ill. A year of

**Had wanted the revolution… He asked if any leading man had.**
stomach pains—neglected or denied—

*secretissime*, **on the quiet. Monroe admits it.**
& he had gone to a specialist who had

**wd. not endow a university (in 1826)**
ordered exploratory surgery & then came

**I said I had no desire that the interruption of social**
the operation that revealed an abdomen ravaged

**Seventy-four years, verge of my birthday, shaking hand**
by cancer so extensively it could not be ameliorated by any excision & removal.

**So this is (may we take it) Mitteleuropa:**
Then came chemotherapy to delay, even if not to ameliorate,

**hebrew affections, in the family, and nearly everything else**
F.'s end—which was estimated at a

**"get an i-de-a, I-mean-a biz-nis i-de-a?"**
year, at most. A tumor was growing on his spine,

**to be sold *a schavezo* at a price as if wholesale**
causing terrible pain. He was at home to stay.

**needing salt, made their peace with Venice**
His law firm, they of the demonstrative callousness with regard to the life, suffering & death of their legal

**A lady asks me**
**I speak in season**
opponents, kindly sent him his pay & paid also

**He is not vertu but cometh of that perfection**
his medical bills, D. told me. I wrote letters to him & she replied.

**He draweth likeness and hue from like nature**
F. spoke with me on the phone—perhaps it was only once.

**Sacrum, sacrum, inluminatio coitu.**
Conversation evoked our early friendship, memorialized it

**"Thou shalt not," said Martin Van Buren, "jail 'em for debt."**
even if inadequately, unbearably, with an intensity of feeling for what could not be

**"if they vote as they are bid by their employers"**
restored because the future had been called off. & he received much less of it than the full year of which his doctor had

**In Europe often by private houses, without assistance of banks**
assured him—perhaps falsely, knowingly falsely,

**"years and nine months, if the charter be not extended…"**
for hope's sake. D. told me

**"Bank curtailed"**
that for a while longer, F. worked in the garden

**Said one of the wool-buyers:**
& maintained the pond & rested on the bench. He liked doing that—just as he'd liked building that patio long ago.

**An' that year Metevsky went over to America del Sud**
But the pain in his back became too great, it prevented such exertions

**Said how useful short sellin' was,**
& his decline put him in bed, or more often in a chair—he

**been waiting since Tiberius' time**
couldn't sleep lying down because of the pain in his back.

**the family was preparing her body for burial**
The words for pain—physical & emotional—are utterly futile.

**Said Herr Krupp (1842): guns are a merchandise**
Are there antonyms for pain that can make the mere sound of words
into a little balm? It was in those last months

**Opposite the Palace of the Schneiders**
or weeks, when he was an invalid, that we spoke by telephone.
His voice had changed, too,

**Desolate is the roof where the cat sat**
weakened & changed & hurt

**First honey and cheese**
by the disease. D. told me F. was using

**Always with your mind on the past....**
his computer to work on poems; to lessen physical strain, I

**Beaten from flesh into light**
guessed. (But the after-years went by & I never got
to see the poems.) & after F. died, I was shaken by her telling me
that he'd said I'd been his closest friend.
I felt I had been terribly inadequate.
Once in a great while, in after times, I would take from my
shelves the *Cantos* of our shared student days—the clipped, concise
brilliance of description, the lovely
rhythms & sounds of words, the beautiful evocations of
ancient & other worlds, the overbearing eccentricity & intolerable political
insanity, the elevated ideals of the experience of reading & of

writing poetry, the putrid fascism, the disillusionment,
the propagandizing, the self-promotion,
the profound
errors of

**Esprit de corps in permanent bodies**
judgment, the history-steeped or politically poisoned peculiarities

**"Taking advantage of emergency" (that is war)**
of opinion, Pound's love of imagistic clarity & his

**ÀGALMA, haberdashery, clocks, ormoulu, brocatelli**
bent for moral ugliness, his delight in the echoes of ancient & modern

**Past Xrestes, a great river**
languages & his willful folly, his bumbling linguistic jokeyness,
his imprisonment, his

**Their men clomb up the crags**
ambiguous repentance & sorrow, his

**"Ma Questo," said the Boss, "è divertente."**
acquiescence to dying—as Pound believed he would experience it

**"Where the Pope goes is lack of money"**
or as others perceived it or as others made use of it on

**Renewal of higher life**
Pound's behalf as a lesser indignity than being hanged for genuine treason—

**"Don't waste time having ideas"**
& his return to Italy, the years of abstaining

**expense of the tax in collection is therefore**
from life, from light, the recantation of the whole artistic project,
the descent into

**"We ought, I think, to say in civil terms: You be damned"**
silence, the legendary sweep of the whole career,

**be lent to whomso can best use it USE IT**
the status of outliving his own renown or infamy, the adorers &

> was sent months ago to YYour HHighness AA VV a memorial

the revilers, the end... all of that given to the poet who lived such a long life,
while for the simpler, more agonizing, more compelling contradictions of my
friend the span was—had been—so short,

> commanding their will, we humbly with reverence

& who, like me, lived nothing so extravagant as Pound's range of experience
& passions & grievous errors, of artistic triumphs & failures. Sun & leaves
made a back-&-forth dappling of light & shade over the chess game, the
handwritten drafts or sketches of poems, & in that time we easily drifted in
self-excuse while keeping our ambitions to ourselves,
but also we failed to forgive

> whereof December was the x th month and

ourselves for the worlds we had not deliberately been made in—
we, like everyone else, had been formed in the inescapable spaces
of family & struggle & hopes.

> get that straight—capital two hundred thousand

A blessed gentle breeze soughs through the limbs
of the leafy tree that stands over our thinking.
We drink strong tea; we smoke

> To the serenissimo Dno (pronounced Domino)

one luxurious cigarette each of black tobacco; I move a knight; he, a bishop;

> having chief place and desire that the

near us, in the acacia shade, we have a few books of poems,
some of them open;

> St. George, two hokey-pokey stands and the unicorn

our table & chairs stand unevenly on the gravel of the narrow

> in the parish of San Giovanni (Joannis)

short driveway of the redwood cottage;

> with its own magistrates, its own ministers

& Leo, the kitten M. & I adopted, is looking at us through one
of the yellow framed windows or,

> payable every two months had been 8 and 1/2

the year before, Buster (named by F.), the calmly authoritative

**but only for civil debts, that it serve not as a safe cache for criminals**
street cat turned affectionate when

**which attain to the Office of Grasslands**
we took him in—but unable to resist fighting—& who, as at night,

**And thou shalt not, Firenze 1766, and thou shalt not**
is lying on the roof of the cottage & watching us & watching too for
feline enemies. He lived by tooth & claw, & though he seemed hale,
would die of bite-transmitted disease.

**also singing the litanies**
But now in memory he's still sleeping half in the gentle sun

**or else outside Siena. This was a law called**
& half in the soothing shade. Cat's paradise

**Premier Brumaire: Vous voudrez citoyen**
is nearly ours, too, in our sort-of-Mediterranean
moment when F. stirs from languid thought & suddenly moves another

**Wherewith I pay God, Madam my sister and cousin,**
chess piece; perhaps this morning G. will show up from

**that split common property among tillers;**
down the street, full of cheer & his entertaining

**With *Usura***
expressions & wry skepticism, or we will go to his house & play

**nor Pier della Francesca; Zuan Bellin' not by usura**
ping-pong at his backyard table in another perpetually or even eternally

**And if you will say that this tale teaches…**
sunny & Edenic day. The industrial clouds & swamps, the stinks & waste
lands, of northern New Jersey are likely also to have condemned F.'s body
to fatal pain & exhaustion by toxins, to have harmed him early before
he would enjoy

**war, I don't think (or have it your own way)**
his hale Californian strength—"mens sana in corpore sano," he
liked to say. Occasionally F. or G. or I would pluck a ripe plum from

       **"They are mendacious, but if the tribe gets together"**
the tree overhead between ping-pong games, & we talked of poems, of

       **of the first phase of this opus, Mr. Marx, Karl, did not**
       words, of Davie, of Davie on Pound, of our own

       **helandros   kai heleptolis   kai helarxe**
       never-to-be-written "cantos" that would never

       **Who even dead, yet hath his mind entire!**
achieve either a historical sweep or a depth of interiority, a breadth

       **Wheat shoots rise new by the altar**
       or a pungency, a humaneness or a world

       **His wing-print is black on the roof tiles**
of beautiful detail, & in that sense our imagined work
would be unlike the great flawed book by the horribly
       flawed poet.
       This very book on my shelf.

       **KAI MOIRAI' ADONIN**
**When the almond bough puts forth its flame,**
**When the new shoots are brought to the altar**
       My friend, how I miss you now!


       F.  ~  1945-1992

**Note on "Elegy"**

Almost always I am slow at writing. On May 29, 1996, writing as fast as I could, trying to complete—for myself, as a memorial gesture rather than as a draft of new work—an account of my friend F., several years after his death, I wrote out in brown ink, in the margins of my first copy (bought in 1970) of *The Cantos of Ezra Pound*, an improvised remembrance. I wrote from the title page (beginning under the title) till on p. 239 I happened to complete what I was trying to articulate, using mostly the space of the top page margins, sometimes writing down one side of the page, too, and also under the final lines when, as at the end of some *Cantos*, the printed text on a particular page left more space. The book seemed to need more marks in it to serve as the futile tokens that I was adding to it to make present, a little, the absence of the friend whom this same copy had once served. Later, on nearly every page I made a small drawing in black India ink or I glued a small piece of colored paper or a fragment of a larger drawing. Then I put the book on a shelf.

Twelve years after I had done this, my friend and the book returned to my thoughts and I wondered what the first line of each page of the *Cantos* might be saying in a chance dialogue with what I had written—a dialogue I myself had fixed in place but to which I had never listened. That is, I wondered what might be said if I were to listen to the first lines on each page of the *Cantos*, incorporating them, montaging them, into my hand-written narrative. After all, I was merely adding something to Pound's original montage. If mine had been grief-writing, Pound's was too, in a sense—mine entirely for a friend, Pound's partly for European civilization and American history (as he—crotchety, quirky, brutally right-wing—believed). I took the book down from a high shelf and looked at it again. In my haste in 1996 I had inadvertently skipped a few pages, and on every page after 239 I had only drawn a wavy brown line across the top margin. I think I had kept marking those pages even if only with a streak of ink because although I hadn't been able to recuperate any more of the story of which I was reminding myself, or of my feelings about it, or couldn't articulate even one word more, I had felt that I had to keep marking till I finished the book again, so to speak—extending my marks as a kind of rejection of the book (for complicated reasons) that was at the center of the story I wanted to tell. So I then typed out what my handwriting and Pound's typographer's first lines of the *Cantos* pages happened to compose when read together.

The Pound of the *Cantos*, playing with language, form, allusion, and poetic thinking among the great dead, but having botched much of this work with appalling attitudes, was himself one among several tutelary poetic figures among the great dead in the reading and discussing that F. and I frequently shared when we were students—he working on English poetry and his own poems, I on poems, translations, and the history of modern poetry in English and Romance languages.

In 1996, in partnership with the superb classicist Charles Segal, I was about to begin working on a translation of Euripides' *Bakkhai*, and I rescued my undergraduate Greek grammar—a relic of my failure to keep up with other students learning the language—and I began studying commentaries and existing translations of that ancient drama. When F. and I had been together in graduate school, he had translated some of Horace. F.'s Horace and my own later work in Greek were among our own Poundian poetic gestures of poetic self-making. How uncanny it seems to me that I should have run out of words and into my silent wavy line at the end of Canto XLVII, in which—bringing both F. and me as close to his work as anything could—Pound revels in Homer and ancient Mediterranean myth, in his intuition for mapping modern experience onto ancient accounts, and in the imagistic vigor and the emphatic rhythms of his lines at their best.

When I quote one of Pound's lines with end-punctuation, I retain that punctuation. I have corrected a few omissions and redundancies and errors of fact in my account, and restored a few additional smaller memories that returned to me when working on this memorializing of a friendship cut short. The pagination of the *Cantos* is that of the first edition of 1970. The spaces between passages mark the movement onto each new page of the *Cantos*.

**Reginald Gibbons** was born in Houston and grew up there. He studied Romance Languages at Princeton and Comparative Literature at Stanford. He has taught creative writing at Columbia University, Princeton, Northwestern, Warren Wilson, and elsewhere. His novel *Sweetbitter* won the Anisfield-Wolf Book Award from the Cleveland Foundation and the Texas Institute of Letters Jesse Jones Award for Best Novel. It was reprinted in paperback by Penguin, then by LSU Press, and a third time by JackLeg Press. Gibbons' two books of short/"flash" fiction are *Five Pears or Peaches* (Broken Moon Press) and *An Orchard in the Street* (BOA Editions). *Three Poems* is his twelfth book of poems. His *Creatures of a Day* (LSU Press) was a Finalist in poetry for the National Book Award. He has won fellowships from the Guggenheim Foundation, the National Endowment for the Arts, and the Fulbright Program (Spain). The cover art of *Three Poems* is a watercolor by Gibbons. Gibbons was the editor of *TriQuarterly Magazine* (Northwestern University) from 19781 till 1997. His translations include Mexican poets (in New Writing from Mexico, a special issue of *TriQuarterly*; the poetry of Luis Cernuda (Univ. of California Press), poems of Jorge Guillén (co-translated with Anthony L. Geist, Princeton Univ. Press); Ilya Kutik's selected poems, *The Wasp of Time*, and also Sophocles' *Selected Poems: Odes and Fragments* (Princeton Univ. Press), Euripides' *Bakkhai*, and Sophocles' *Antigone*. With Ilya Kutik, Gibbons has also co-translated Ilya Kutik's selected poems, *The Wasp of Time*; and also with Kutik, has completed a collection of selected poems of Boris Pasternak and another of Marina Tsvetaeva.

www.ingramcontent.com/pod-product-compliance
Lightning Source LLC
Chambersburg PA
CBHW020343170426
43200CB00006B/494